A Lifetime of Reflections
Laura Crean

ISBN 978–1–4478–6620-6

http://lauracrean-artist-writer-poet.webs.com/

Contents

Poem   Page

The Age of Faith Part Two

Home and Family (Age 30-38)

Kids and Chaos

Not Just a Mum!

The Journey Continues

Last Thoughts

Since I was a child I have used poetry as an expression
of my inner life, composing verses reflecting my
childhood memories, emotions, spiritual and
environmental contemplations and just general
observations of my family life and the world around me.
I have chosen to compile my poetry in this book of
reflections and have included one of my own paintings
on the front cover (there is a lovely hard back version
full of my own paintings and photo images, beautifully
displayed within its pages). This book is for my family
and friends and anyone who just has a love of the poetic
art form or an interest in the poetry collection of a true
romantic soul spanning 24 years.

X Love and Light X
Laura Crean

Is Anyone out there?

Is anyone out there?
Can you declare
just how you are feeling?
Can you say it fair?

Can you describe your love
to me quite plain?
Can you describe your feelings to me
and still stay sane?

Can you be honest with me
and say you feel anger?
Or will you lie and treat yourself
as you would treat a stranger?

Can you sit quite still
when you say you are happy?
Or will you break down and cry
and just say "Maybe"?

Are you one of these people
who will always say,
"It's bound to get better
on another day"

Or will you stand tall
and cry at the top of your voice,
"I am free to be who I am
and I will make that choice!"

The Age of Innocence
Aged 14 - 18

I call this chapter
'The Age of Innocence',
and as you will see - from a young age
I found a need to write down just little verses
at first, little snippets of thoughts, feelings and
observations. I loved my English lessons at
school and it was then I started to appreciate
the art form that is the written word.

Some of these early poems may seem a little
naive but that is why when I look back on
them now I find them all the more charming in
their innocence.

The Age of Innocence
Part One

Hush Little Child

Hush little child.
I wish that I could
blow away your fears
and brush away your tears,
but I can't.

Be still little child.
I wish that I could
know what it is you are seeing
and feel what it is you are feeling,
but I can't

Don't hide little child.
Shout out all of your confusion,
make your own contribution,
just don't hide.

Hush little child.
I wish that I could
blow away your fears
and brush away your tears,
but I can't.

Hush Little child - Be still.
God alone knows how you feel.

Young at Heart

When children play together
they always seem to say,
"I wish I were grown up
and could do what I want all day.
I want to be an adult
and have my very own home."

But when they get their dream come true
they still feel all alone.
And when they are all adults
and playing's at a cease,
it is really being children
that they truly miss.

The Shepherd Boy

High up on a hilltop
I saw a shepherd boy,
he was watching over a flock of sheep
grazing nearby.

But a lamb looking for adventure
wandered off one day,
the shepherd boy, not noticing
was scolded for his mislay.

Another day went by
and the lamb was still not found
and so the shepherd boy
went searching all around.

But alas my friends, the shepherd boy
he fell crashing to his death,
the lamb was found the next morning
licking the dead boy's face.

And so the Shepherd boy
was buried up on the pasture,
where until its dying day, the lamb would stand by
watching over his master.

**I wrote this poem for an English lesson on bullying at
age 14 and I'm sure if I remember rightly,
my music class chose to use it for our class composition,
which I believe I wrote the music for as well.**

Masquerade

I could still see him through my watery eyes,
I felt for him, he was in disguise.
What a masquerade his life must be,
but although I hurt, inside he was soft I could see.

His friends in the crowd were cheering him on,
as if he were on stage singing a song.
My whole life flashed before my eyes,
maybe it was me who was in disguise.

I think after that I must have blacked out,
because I awoke to hear him shout,
"You've killed her you fool!" the voice was clear,
"No time to cry now, just leave her here!"

The footsteps died.
The bully had cried
for me, the victim of the raid,
I was right, he was living a deadly masquerade.

Infinity

...After Earth - Space
After darkness - silence
After time - extinction
After death - illumination
After Heaven - Earth
After Earth - Space...

Space to Breathe

Although I like the company,
sometimes just the same,
I like to sit alone awhile,
just sit and contemplate.

This rushing, busy world of ours
just seems to go too fast,
so I sit alone in a quiet spot
and watch the world go past.

When I have had enough
of being on my own,
I like to share the company
of everyone at home.

I think we go through stages,
having different needs,
we want to have a point of view
but also space to breathe.

Memories' Sight, Reflected Light

Every time I see a light,
the reflection from some unknown sight,
I imagine from that one glimpse
the memories within it since.

I try to hold it in my mind,
the lighted memory,
not inside the eye
but behind!

What is it about that light -
That shows the past, the present, the future
and life's never-ending plight?

Night Air

I looked up to see the stars so bright,
the moon so full,
the air just right,
the fragrant smell of the flowers and trees
mingled with the dew
and the sound of the sea
lapping on the quiet shore at night,
broken only by a rare cat fight!

I Can't Count Sheep

On a clear night when I can't sleep,
on those nights when I can't seem
to count sheep...

...I stumble out of bed
and out the back door
and breathe the fresh air
that makes me feel awake all the more -
I look up at the beautiful stars in the sky
and I wonder why they don't look as high,
as high as they really, truly are
away out in the universe so far -
And I wonder while I am standing there
about other planets - I wonder and stare,
until I finally feel I can sleep,
now I don't need to waste time counting sheep.

This poem was written for a Religious Education lesson on Mother Theresa. She is one of my personal all time heroes and I was a little bit upset that Princess Diana's funeral drowned out the importance of marking this amazing woman's own, she did so much for the needy and should be remembered always as the Saint that she is.

The Streets of Calcutta

Close your eyes and what do you see?
Food on a table, a house sheltering me.

Open your eyes now what do you see?
A ragger-bone person, this person is me.

My body so weak
My eyes full of sleep
My stomach so hungry
My clothes so cheap.

The ground beneath me cold and hard,
bodies around me yard after yard.

Close your eyes and what do you see?
The great gates of Heaven opening to me.

Open your eyes now what can you tell?
Life all around me, the dark heat of hell.

Looking Ahead

I look ahead,
what do I see?
A feeling of dread,
what can it be?
The feeling it nags,
it tightens, it turns,
it weakens, it sags.
An unsure future
what can it
hold?
To really be sure
I must try and mould
the talent within
so sure and so bold.
Then I must find
the right path ahead
amongst the twists,
the turns, the winds,
perhaps it is the journey
I truly dread!

The Mind's Door

What is happening inside my head?
Am I alive or am I dead?
I know I am alive because I breathe and feel
but inside my head it is all concealed.

My thoughts and consciousness seem to be missing,
I know what is happening in the world
but I am not really listening
I understand and yet I do not,
I feel as if my brain is tied in a knot.

Somewhere in the back of my mind
there is a spark of light I am trying to find,
when I find that light I know what to do,
I must walk into the light
and carry on straight through.

Then I will find what I am looking for,
then it is time to enter
through a new and different door.

Feelings

Loneliness brings about madness or art

Sadness brings about pain

Love brings about peace of mind

And anger just makes you insane!

What is in my eyes?

Look in my eyes

What do you see?

There is depth and there are dreams

belonging to me -

A sparkle of light,

A splash of blue

that show my heart belongs to you.

The Living Fire of Love

Not far from my dying soul

there lies a living fire,

it burns within my heart,

it calls for us to never part -

So burn - my everlasting fire!

Now take heed and listen to your heart

and let that eternal fire burn -

Light that fire, listen to your heart

and I will never leave your side.

Tightrope Life

Take my hand and squeeze it gently,

pull me close and hold me tight,

your eyes always seem haunted,

but I'll keep you safe from the terrors of the night.

Don't let the dark keep you

from walking that straight line,

It's a tightrope so don't look down!

I know sometimes I seem to not notice

that you feel afraid of what lies in store,

But I will always be there when you need me

and we'll walk that straight line together

hand in hand forever more.

Don't let the dark keep you from

walking that straight line

It's a tightrope so don't look down!

Like my very Love...

Like the waves lapping on the shore...

Like the clouds rolling by...

Like a breeze catching at the branches...

Like the ripples of a shower on a pond...

Like the beating of my heart...

Like my soul reaching out to yours...

Like my very love...

The Age of Innocence
Part Two

This poem was written on a boat trip whilst on holiday with my parents in Venice. It seems that even from such a young age there were many times I would just sit and contemplate things. This poem is a testament to such youthful reflective moments.

Ripples of Light

Ripples of light on the surface of the sea,

falling from the edge of the world it may seem,

gulls alight on a wooden perch,

their eyes scanning quickly in an unknown search.

A lonely shack as the sun sinks low,

its owner a fisherman returning slow,

the waters afar try to keep their dark secrets,

the wind whistles its gossip but there is no one to hear it...

Broken Hearts

Take the sun
and move it from the solar system...

We would die

Take the water
and move it from the Earth...

We would die

Take our hearts
and move them from our bodies...

We would die

Take our love
and move it from our hearts...

We would surely die a painful death!

Savour the Moment

Close your eyes and feel

Do not move

Feel the sun's warmth

Listen...

Listen to the sounds
of creation

The birds

The trees

The wind

Hear and feel

yourself

breathe...

Be glad you can

Thank God

you are

Alive

Wisdom and Knowledge

There's a little bit of a philosopher in all of us
even at the tender age of 16!

Throughout our lives we are learning,
there is always something new.
We find in our lives a yearning
for educational doors to go through.

Nobody can know everything,
no matter what they think,
it takes a lot of time and pain
for our brains and knowledge to find that link.

But even if you find knowledge,
that isn't all you need -
Knowledge also needs wisdom
for it to truly breed.

Life's Maze

Sometimes I think our lives
can be like a maze,
it is very confusing
and everything is in a haze.
We are turning new corners
all the time
and unless you meet a dead end,
you go on quite fine.

When you reach the middle,
much like our lives,
you try to get out again -
But just try and get out alive!
It seems like you are trying
for ever and ever,
the turns become more difficult,
your sense of direction never gets any better.

And when you finally
get out of the maze,
you have nowhere to go,
your mind's in a daze;
You try again
to crack that maze
and keep on trying
for the rest of your days.

You only achieve
a brief sense of freedom,
it is never enough
for your heart to feed on;
And so you want the truth as well
and keep on searching
deeper and deeper,
until your life inside the maze
becomes a deadly hell!

The Truth of the Soul

A soul stood before the gates of Time.
The Immortal One asked,
"Do you have a question before you enter?"

The soul asked,
"Father Time, tell me, how do I tell
the truth from a lie?"

This was the Lord of Time's reply;

"The answer is simple -
A lie can disguise itself as the truth
and the truth may often seem too good to be true.
A lie will multiply until it becomes confusion
but the truth will withstand the test of time -
it will always remain constant - no matter what.

The answer is - Time will tell!"

The soul seemed distracted;

"So when I enter through your gates,
the truth will be revealed to me?"

Time answered...

"No! The truth will not be revealed to you.
You will be revealed to the truth,
because
Truth is the master of Time."

Why Me?

Why am I here on this planet of ours?
Why do I do what I do?

How come I make the choices I make?
Which door do I go through?

How did I get here?
Why was I born?

How do I know
if I'll see the next dawn?

How can I hear?
How can I see?

What is the reason?
And why am I me?

The questions we ask
we must answer ourselves,

if we can't find them,
wait till life tells!

Stigmata

"I bear the wounds of Christ!" they say,
but they do not wish it to go away,
it makes them feel special,
they feel like Saints,
the blood and pain cannot drive them to faint.
If the son of God can take the pain,
they ignore the taunts that
should drive a man to shame!

They soon go, they do disappear,
returning at Easter, a time to be revered.
The palm of hand,
the sole of foot,
which side was that spear put?
No one knows!
But the mind reveals what the pictures show.

In every church that shows him on the cross
the wounds reappear to the willing host.
The stigmata
a blessing or a curse
from the Holy Ghost?

Lonely Secrets

A teardrop glistens
in the corner of your eye,
why are you so distant?
Why can't you cry?
What are you hiding
in those dark pools?
Why are you abiding
by some strange
and secret rules?

I have tried to reach you
over so many years
but you are still too lonely
to release the flow of tears.

Independent and stubborn
obviously from birth
something makes you yearn
for everything you're worth.

So I keep on striving
to find that secret there,
the one your mind is hiding,
the one I wish you'd share.

The Healing Heart

True healing comes from within
and needs four things
to do its job properly.

Truth, trust, love and time.

If you are true to yourself
then all other truths will follow.

Trust is a hard thing to give
and an even harder thing to gain
but without it
there is no hope or faith.

True love can only be received
if it is given freely.
Firstly you must learn to love yourself
from the inside.
"He who only half breathes, half lives"
It isn't enough to concentrate on the physical side
of your 'being'
As everyone finds something
about their physical life unsatisfactory.
If you can learn to love both your inner and outer selves
as two reflections of the one soul
then you will find balance in your life.
Then you will be able to share your love completely.

Finally time.
Time is the ultimate truth and the ultimate healer.
Be patient. Have faith.
And know that you are loved and appreciated
by the divine spirit of God.

Above all
Follow your heart.

Dreamer of Unconsciousness

I feel alone, I feel confused
I wander aimlessly bemused.
I feel afraid, I feel so wise
I share the power behind those eyes.

I saw the light, I felt ashamed
I feel inside that I am maimed.
I dreamt the dream of Paradise
yet burnt the stare of pure cold ice.

And so a wanderer
on the plains of death,
I awake to feel the strength
of a lover's breath.

My wishing Star

I feel my eyes floating

towards that distant star

as a very tiny wish

follows it afar

"Where are you going

and where will you stop?

Will my wish catch up with you

before you start to drop?"

Down and down and down to Earth

falls that wishing star

a gentle, quiet landing

way off in the dark.

But although it's landing

quiet as it seems

It doesn't really land you know

only in our dreams.

**I've always been drawn by the beauty of the sea,
even before I was lucky enough to live by it!**

The Sea

A ripple, a bubble,
a whirlpool of light,
this body so clear
but deep out of sight,
the motion of movement
slowed in its course
because of this
shape changing
body of force.

Its action so soothing,
unpolluted it cures
but when unprotected,
its victims it lures,
it can be quite violent
and swallow you whole
but it will always
look after its own.

The creatures it harbours
range from tiny to beast
but all it is asking
is to leave it in peace.

Always Together

Somehow at night
when we are apart
I feel the strong and loving
beat of your heart.

In the darkness
in my sleep
I share your tears
and with you I weep.

I know you are lonely
I feel your pain
and the simple reason why I know
is because I feel the same.

The Truest Love

When someone's love embraces you
and you embrace them back,
you find that love comes seeping through
into one big emotional trap.

You try so hard to just hold on
you want this love to last
and soon you find yourself clinging
to that ever loving past.

But if your love's a true one
the clinging you will not need,
for the truest love
will forever more succeed.

The Wheel of Life

I think life is like a wheel

it keeps on turning round

and like a wheel

you can turn it forward

turn it back

or keep it still.

But if life was like a wheel

and time could be controlled

What mysteries

and treasures

the wheel of life

would hold.

Time

I see a clock ticking
in my mind's eye,
it is so big
it fills the very sky,
the tick, tick, ticking
of time's pendulum
makes me wonder
if my future has already begun.

The hands keep turning
on that heavenly clock,
when oh when
will time ever stop?
Why do I feel like time
is dragging me down?
And why can time's silence
never be found?

I wish I lived
where time did not exist
then I wouldn't have to make
a daily, timed
routine of a list.

Do Only Good

Do only good in all you do,
be faithful, honest, kind and true,
to heal with love, good will and faith
this road you'll always travel safe.

Any deeds performed with heart,
with pure intentions from the start,
a hundred times and more they will return
and in your heart forever burn.

But if you choose
to hurt or hex,
such negativity
will vex
and only darkness
in your heart you'll hold
be sure it will return
threefold!

This poem was partly inspired by a dream I had
but also it grew from a feeling and then an idea for a
story -
but out of it all came this poem - and
I have to say it is one of my favourites.

The Circle of Truth

I sit within the circle
the circle of truth
amid a swarm of faces
who never give out proof.

I try to look around me
but cannot quite focus on
what is behind the circle's edge
the truth that lies beyond.

And now begins the lesson
the reason children sit
within the circle's world of dreams
where they so neatly fit.

The subject of the lesson
is to control what is within
to capture our true innocence
and disregard all sin.

Each child sits in the middle
their essence to be found
the mind and soul a riddle
around each life is wound.

Now I stand in the circle
all eyes are turned to me
I must release the power
and set my spirit free.

I know I will awake soon
the circle will be gone
and all the children with it
but we will always be as one.

As you can probably tell by now
there are a few obvious themes to my poetry.
Even in the early years they generally had
a rather philosophical thread
and intertwined with these enquiring characteristics
I developed an environmental concern.
This in turn became the beginnings of a spiritual
journey which started to look outward as well as inward
and led to an interest in science, psychology, cosmology
and also gave me a real passion for ancient history,
myths and legends.

Ending

Why do I feel that
the end is so near?
I don't know how
and I don't know what year,

but something tells me
that the end is so near,
it is something I smell
and something I hear.

The animal's movements
all so tense.
The Earth's ozone barrier
as close as a fence

between our world
and disaster beyond,
through that hole all life
of which we are so fond

is sucked away
into darkness so bold,
far away into
God's strong hold.

Judgment Day

Stop killing the planet people!

This world once clean and beautiful
but now so dull and pitiful
lacks the love of the human race
who cares for nothing and no place.

There is no place upon this Earth
where anyone can show their worth
there is nowhere safe or sacred now
each acre torn apart somehow.

Our planet that for eons showed us love
must now prepare for a broken heart
because of what we have done
on the surface above.

"The end is near!"
some people say,
everyone fears for
Judgment day.

The Age of Fantasy
Aged 19-24

This chapter is self-explanatory - my mother would probably say this is where I live - in a Fantasy world! I would probably have to agree with her!

The Age of Fantasy
Part one

Stark Naked

**I was asked to write a poem as a follow on from
'Masquerade',
this poem turned out quite dark!**

There was nothing in those eyes of his,
dark pits of simple nakedness,
with a wicked, evil, laughing twist.

The pupil,
A black hole of infinity
with no remorse and no pity.

There was nothing to hide his angry woe,
it has churned his mind
and burned his soul.

No one could save him now,
his mind has turned
there is no way out.

His eyes have a stark naked look
of a true and bitter end
most foul!

Realm of Shadows

I closed my eyes and found a place
where I could lose myself in sleep,
no longer doomed to watch the face,
the dreaded hands of destiny to keep
its slow and steady, infinite pace.

In the realm of shadows
time has not the same intentions,
you may sit undisturbed in quiet meadows
or just be a part of the dream's inventions,
observing, partaking or even moulding
its timelessness to your own ends.

Shadows by their nature follow the real;
holding, copying, mirroring their partner's actions;
often though the truth it bends,
its distorted path of time can be a distraction,
like the shadow that is extended with the path of the moon!

So it may seem that time has indeed won -
but the realm will not be conquered so soon.
I must take care not to get completely lost,
this place of dreams is a place to observe
and react accordingly, being careful that the boundaries
crossed
are straight and true and do not swerve
from the path of this reality
to intrude on the realm of confusion!

It is easy to lose your way
in a realm filled with shadows and illusions,
but I know that I can be sure by the light of day
this journey will draw its own conclusions.

Look to the Shadows

Shadows aren't always in darkness,
shadows are half dark half light,
they are not therefore completely hidden
but they can hide the truth from our sight.

So when I say look to the shadows,
it is only to seek what is true,
where you choose to look is your own fate
but be careful to think it right through.

Is your glass half full or half empty?
What do you see when you look in your heart?
If you seek to find order in chaos,
be sure that you know where to start.

The universe was never created,
it simply exists to exist
and as it exists in perfection
so your soul must try and resist
the search for the source of all power
it simply will never be found,
instead seek the wisdom of flowers
and listen to each earthly sound.

The pattern of life is the answer,
the symmetry hiding in space,
like the form of a spiritual dancer
or a tiger whose mastered the chase.

Everything has a reflection,
its opposite and perfect mate,
some may be hiding in shadows
but that's just their natural state.

So be careful what powers you ask for,
ask first, "What do I wish to achieve?"
Do not seek to unbalance nature,
do not seek to abuse or deceive.

Instead look for the beauty and innocence,
for the power in your heart that is pure,
then what is hidden in shadows will start to make sense,
you will then have found darkness a cure.

When seeking the truth in the shadows,
be sure that it wants to be found,
asking the universe too many questions
will only result to confound.

Shadows are there for a reason,
they balance the light and the dark,
know that each month has its season
and each soul leaves a permanent mark.

The Age of Fantasy
Part Two

The Sorceress of Words

A writer sits at writing desk
to begin a spellbound quest -
The jumbled letters
on the magical page
change their meaning
Age by age.

The Sorceress
of word and rune
can conjure up
A nymph of Earth
or Mermaid and Neptune.

Her incantation
weaves a trance,
it sends its reader
on a journey
of mystery
dreams
and chance

Goddess of Illusion

Imagine in your mind's eye
A goddess, to tempt, fascinate, entice...
Her feminine charm allusive yet pure,
suggestive, she calls to allure.

Beyond illusion, vales of mist,
she tempts you closer to embrace and kiss...
She always hovers close yet too far,
delighting eyes to mystify, alarm...

Her enigmatic, deceptive endeavour
will deem her every being
A dream
Forever!

I am fascinated by the idea of time travel
and also the idea of alternate realities.
I love characters from TV like Samuel Becket and
Doctor Who and novels like
The Time Machine by H G Wells.
I love to use my imagination to speculate
what a time traveller might get up to
and what amazing time lines or parallel universes
they may find themselves visiting.
I have even written a novel about time travel
and some Doctor Who fan fiction.

The Time Traveller

Past, present and future,
he will traverse through time,
endlessly turning the treadmill
along that periphery line.
Balancing on the junction
of that temporal wheel,
knowing not its function
or which pathway it will steal.

He is but a wanderer,
enduring age by age
the everlasting conundrum
he faces at each stage.
Although he is immortal
and can forever race the clock,
passing through each portal
he must avoid a paradox.

And so facing this enigma
he has to watch his step,
he must learn to be proficient
treating time with skill and respect.
And if while on this journey
he can do some good
by altering what might have been
then I think he should.

Sea of Serenity

Whilst travelling across the vastness of a desolate moor
I happened upon a lonely sight indeed.
Such a picture to cast a spell and my heart allure,
A gypsy Nymph on her magical steed.

This mystical enchantress with fire in her eyes
held me captivated like a fool.
Such a spirit of nature any human maiden would despise,
her charm and wand were her only tools.

Here I stopped, dismounted, approached with curiosity,
mesmerised by the amulet embedded in her wand.
It was of purest moonstone, the wind whispered,
"Sea of Serenity"
and they seemed to share the closest bond.

I gazed at this translucent orb,
its simplicity marred by a single rune.
It seemed as if all light it had absorbed
and reflected back to our own New Moon.

Then this nomadic beauty
held up the talisman,
in a voice so distant and dreamy
she reflected in Romany tongue,

"I have stolen away the moonlight
because it has been stained,
by looking down upon man's plight
and long seen evil reign.

So now I can return it
from whence it did begin,
The moonstone has cleansed and made it fit
and banished all man's sin."

Then I was alone again
upon that desolate moor.
The enchantress and the moonstone,
no dream I swear I saw.

I believe every soul has the power to create the perfect world, however young or innocent they may be...

Heaven's in your Hand

Each child holds the world in an open hand
to mould it into any shape they choose,
they have a lifetime to understand
that they just can't lose.
They must let their imaginations fly
and be creatively inspired,
if only every child could try
to create the world they each desired...
Imagine the possibilities
and how such a world could be -
a choice of infinite realities,
it could be truly heavenly.
It isn't just a day-dream,
we can make our dreams come true,
it isn't as hard as it may seem,
Heaven is in all of you.
You already hold Heaven in your hand
and also in your heart.
If every child could make a stand
that would be a start.

The Unicorn's Charm

A beautiful being, enchantingly pure,
as white as a lily, so proud and so sure.
With silvery mane that flows in the breeze
and eyes that bewitch you and make your soul freeze.

But in an instant her eyes seem to change
and so melts the ice, causing feelings so strange.
Straight to your heart the warmth travels - but slow
and both captive and unicorn seem to shine and to glow.

Here something passes between the two like a trance,
causing Dryad and Nymph to awaken and dance.
The unicorn's talisman, that pearly white horn
that this beast of perfection is chosen to adorn

works such a spell of pure conjuration
that no mage of sorcery could ever imagine.
The very embroidery of time has no power over her charm,
but she will never maim, hurt or harm,

For she is the truest meaning of good
and reigns as Queen in the
mystical, magical enchanted wood.

I often write about very insubstantial things,
like dreams and metaphysical concepts.
It is in all our natures to contemplate such
philosophical meanderings but romantic souls
like me try and capture such moments, write
them down and keep them for posterity. One
day I pray that someone may read my little
moments of esoteric musings
and be uplifted of spirit.

Flight of Fancy

Why is it when I try to concentrate my thoughts
strange fantasies and dreams leak out?

A childhood memory of favourite toy or game,
a trip to the beach, a best friend - what was her name?

A favourite book whose characters are always heroes who
fight for good and win.

A song - the last one heard - the tone gets stuck inside my
head and it haunts me until I hear another - then that one
will annoy me!

Not realising I was humming to myself,
all eyes on the bus turn in my direction!

A scene from a movie - the best in ts day,
but now the corny sets and bad acting are collectable.

Sometimes a daydream catches me unawares,
one minute talking to a friend...

...and the next a daydream pops into my head
and out of nowhere I start drifting on a sea of memories.

What is a daydream?

A welcome distraction from the harsh realities of daily life
that's all!

Dreams of Flight

I have had the most satisfying dream
since childhood beyond my memory,
the truth behind it and what it really means
is quite a mystery to me.

I have not had the dream of late
since the responsibility of adulthood arrived,
perhaps the innocence and childlike state
is what keeps such dreams alive.

Dreams of flight
a childish fancy perhaps,
always in a star filled sky at night
a time when I can lapse
into a blissful state of warmth, comfort and security,
a time any babe newly born
from the womb can so relate,
it signifies such innocence, such purity.

Perhaps I am re-living a time
before my birth,
a time when the love of my mother
was all life's worth.

Or perhaps it was a premonition
of what is waiting beyond the grave,
the mere tinge of a sensation
a soul released from its body can brave.

Or were they just simple dreams
of innocence
in a world where childish whims
die all too soon?

In dreams of flight we can all sense
the freedom and independence
that we brought with us
from the womb.

Generation 2000

What of my children's future
in the next millennium?
Will they love and nurture the Earth
as its true custodians?
Do they want to clean up this planet
and achieve world peace?
If they don't want the bomb they can ban it
after all the Earth's only on lease.
Is it too much to ask to achieve such goals
in only a thousand years?
Generation 2000 has many roles
to play, it doesn't have time for tears!
Will they struggle to get by
as wars rage on?
Will children continue to die?
Will World Leaders continue to con?
It is hard to be optimistic
when a bomb extinguishes a baby's life
just because two countrymen can't be realistic
or agree to differ peacefully to stop the trouble and strife.
As the planet starts to heat up
and the forests are daily consumed
will the ozone's protection just suddenly stop
and will the planting of trees be resumed?
Will the greenhouse effect become a reality?
Will the Earth suffer another flood?
What will become of humanity?
Will the Earth become an ocean of blood?

The future is just around the corner,
it is approaching fast,
and there is no one to warn her
that the present will soon be the past.
The governments spend too much money
on space flights and weapons of war,
when their sights should be set on the Earth's worries
and its children knocking on death's door.
How can they live such wealthy lives
knowing that half the world suffers?
They continue to lie, cheat, take bribes
and use their own people as buffers.
So let's get our lives in perspective
and help our children achieve
a new generation of humanity, irrespective
of colour and creed.
Let's give this planet an overhaul
so that our children can say,
"Our parents loved us enough to call
a halt to the fear and dismay."
Let the future be colourful
Let the future be bright
Let the future be wonderful
and bring us into the light.

O Stars My Stars

O stars my stars how clearly you shine,
forever bright forever mine
guiding all who travel by night
keeping the world within God's sight.
O stars my stars oblivious of time
to reach your great height I shall not have to climb
for your heavenly light on Earth is sublime
in my lover's eyes tonight.
O stars my stars how can I define?
Your beautiful existence is surely divine,
who has such resistance to your fated design?
Your charm and enchantment will always be there to
remind.
O stars my stars as you look down
on this fragile Earth that is spinning around in space
can you see its worth?
Can you hear each sound it makes on land and surf?
Did you see when its heart started to pound?
Did you witness its birth and did it astound?
O stars my stars can you see our plight?
Have you noticed our struggle?
How life has to fight
to survive? What a muddle!
Does man have the right
to destroy, as we huddle
together on this Earth
to whom we are bound so tight?
O stars my stars will we ever reach you?
Can we ever escape
this planet we're bound to?
Who knows how our future will shape
if our race will get through
the great mound of mistakes it has made.
Payment is due for the damage man's left in his wake.

This poem belongs with a novel I have written called
'Dawn's Greeting' and it is about a collection of beings
called 'Dawn Children' scattered about the universe all
born with the gift to travel through time.
The Heroine is the first 'Dawn Child' to be born on
Earth and the book is the story of her discovery of this
gift. This poem takes the form of a prayer with an
unusual Trinity -
Father Time - Mother Earth - Children of the Dawn

Children of the Dawn
Father
Time
in Heaven
wherever that may be
in whatever form or reality
grant us a diversion from your continuity
give us all a little peace to savour your piety
and the sight of wisdom to travel your road with dignity.

Mother Earth so patient and tolerant of our sins
take away the chains of greed and give your children wings
to fly from our short-sightedness and plant the seeds of
hope
may they blossom with love and charity and help lost souls
to cope.

Children of the Dawn greet the day anew
absorb the bright sun's energies and savour every view
Lend a helping hand to keep the stars from falling
to be the hands of destiny is your only calling.

Yours is the road less travelled
it is the road of time
help us now to plan our route
that leads to the
Divine

The Tree

I have often wondered about the tree,
about how it hears and how it sees,
I have often wondered how it does perceive
the world through roots and bark and leaves.
It is so old and wise and full of trust,
it stands alone surveying its surrounding space.
Then we invade its privacy because we must
furnish our homes and show we have good taste.
And so with pine and the great wise Oak,
a cabinet, a chest of drawers and such
are crafted with an ancient skill that is no joke,
but do we really need to build so much?
And in our search for such material wealth,
have we not forgotten our true friend the tree?
Who is the reason for our good health
purifying the very air we breathe!
What will happen to our "superior race"
when we have chopped down the very last tree?
Will we be able to keep up our present pace?
Will we still be alive and breathing free?
The tree was here before our race began to abuse
this planet's great and wealthy store
and yet this environmental disaster seems to amuse
Man, the caretaker - who rapes the Earth, craving more!
Will man ever stop to take stock
of the Earth's depleting supply?
He has ransacked this planet for its heart, the clock
is slowly and surely ticking as time goes by.

Opening the Star-gate

As above, so below
the signs are there for all to know
unlock the gate with the key of time
over Saturn's threshold lies your way and mine.
Orion's clue to the soul's heavenly journey
is encoded in the myths of Man's ancient memory.
And so from Khufu to Peter's reign,
the new custodian of the secret of the same...
Jesus knew the message he should teach,
a new age, another chance for heaven the soul to reach.
But the Son of Man is not all he seems,
he is the first and the last, the Alpha and Omega,
so what for mankind could this possibly mean?
At the beginning of the Age of the Dawn of Adam
from the east the Lion reared his royal head,
at the end of the Age, The Guardian of Time
now comes forth in the Lion's stead.
To complete the cycle of Orion's reign
we must heed the signs in that heavenly chain
and watch for the opening of that symbolic gate
and the Earth shattering changes it may create.
Now is the ending but also the start
of a new chain of time and a new change of heart.
We must now unlock that magical door
hope is the key but only time can be sure...
that we may learn from all our mistakes,
Time is the journey the soul must take.

The Tower

Why is it that since Man began to build,
the bricks and mortar have become a status symbol?
As if continuing to grow, they are so willed
and beneath its spire all are humble.
It is a symbol of great power
to be a higher being above all others.
To climb the heights of his great Tower
is to reach Heaven before his brothers.
Some men get lost when on this great journey,
locked in that ivory tower of seclusion.
They continue in their search, all the while learning
their "towering intellect" is just an illusion.
As Man observes the view from his skyscraper
his perspective is altered with his height,
these man made mountains cast such shadows
it does hamper the truth of what exists below,
for it is out of sight!
And this is why all men of power in church or castle
from spire or turret do survey
the happenings below them that are distorted,
all are carried with the screen of clouds - away!
Why is it that in dreams we continue climbing
the never ending spiral stair?
Never really truly finding
what it is we are looking for up there.

The higher up we carry on our tiring climb
the brighter shines that cleansing light
and running out of precious time
it is too late to descend back to unwanted night.
And when awaking exhausted from the climbing dream,
the taste of "more" lingers in the air.
We have touched the gates to Heaven, it may seem
and all that's left is an ache of wanting to resume our
journey there.
Sometimes in our climbing dream
we may lose our balance and start to fall,
only finding when we continue dreaming
we have begun again the climb up that steep wall.
Where does the climbing search for power end
and is it to be reached through building towers?
Or is it only in the dreams of men
and the search for Heaven between lovers?

The Age of Faith
Age 25 - 28

So as you can see by now, as the new
Millennium began my thoughts and feelings
became more and more philosophical.
The World seemed to be more and more
gripped with fears and insecurities about the
end of the world. Disaster films, prophecies
and the New Age Movement were springing up
left, right and centre -
and so my poems reflected this trend in
thinking and in my personal life I began to
start to have a longing for something in my life
that I couldn't seem to put my finger on.
People often call this empty feeling the
'God shaped hole'!
So as I came closer and closer in my search for
God, my poems started to change shape
somewhat - you have already seen this in some
of the previous poems. I hope you enjoy the
rest of them in this chapter.

Love and Light
X Laura X

The Age of Faith
Part One

Disaster Junkies

The TV screen flickers,
its pictures seem nonsensical, meaningless.
The newscaster offers no emotion concerning
the welfare of the souls involved. So much news,
so commonplace it is mundane.
An earthquake here, a tidal wave there,
a war, a crime, just a headline!
Current affairs, something of interest?
Or a 'current affair', a person of power caught unawares?
Their public apologies seem so blasé,
who cares as long as it's there not here,
I'm not wasting time shedding a tear
for a story that returns year after year!
A community of disaster junkies show a casual indifference
and surf the net, zombies of technology.
Every new movie competes for top spot and reflect
doomsday views of the ticking of the apocalyptic clock,
but the end never comes...
Here I sit flicking through the channels, not really
watching,
but it seems like an appropriate replacement for company.
The newscaster, a familiar stranger
keeps me informed of what isn't really important to me.
It doesn't pay my rent or offer a hand of comfort,
but it is a window, albeit one that is closed to me..
The TV screen flickers,
the pictures fade into the decor of the room,
the sound of a weeping survivor of a flood
is drowned by the laughter of my baby.
She watches the colours on the screen with interest
already hypnotized by the 'dreaded box' -
the next generation of TV addict glued to the telly.
I hope the cartoons improve!

The Universal Language

What language does nature use
to try and communicate?
What accent does it choose
to explain to us our fate?

It is a secret language
the language of the ancient ones,
it is easy for gods to brandish
the sword of truth
spoken in such foreign tongues!

So is it Hebrew or Egyptian?
Is it Hindi, French or Greek?
Is it the language of the China man,
the ancient Celtic or the Sikh?

It is not of any culture
that was invented by Mankind,
it is the language of the number
of the secret name of everything
that Man has yet to find.

It is the number shown in patterns,
of the perfect, natural state,
it is the number of reflections
and the heartbeat's constant rate.

It is the pattern and the rhythm
of the cycle of the moon,
it is the internal clock within
us all that hints of impending doom.

Number takes on many forms
and is the ultimate design
of everything in the universe -
it is the language of the divine.

Universal Mystery

What is it that my heart is searching for?

It is something I cannot see or hear and yet it is something
more,
a distant shape and a gentle echo that I hold most dear.
Reflections in a moonlit pond, in mists and dew-kissed
meadows.
Nature's silent song and the spirit's secret shadows.

What is it that is just beyond my grasp?

It is something I cannot taste or smell
and yet it is a familiar flavour that is on the tip of my
tongue
and fading from my memory fast.
The fragrance of a perfume that I know but cannot name,
the smell of distant memories linger in a room
but no one is to blame.

What is it that my soul is yearning for?

It is just around the corner, out of sight but behind an open
door.
It is the memories of things to come
and the future of things that once were.
The secret name of everything that lives within our sight,
the power of the word, Man has abused this sacred right!
But however hard he whispers his abuse,
you can be sure that God has heard
and that Man has tightened his own noose!

What is it that is just beyond my reach?

It is the unimagined,
it is the hopes and fantasies
that my dreams are there to try and teach.
It is the hidden wisdom that we ourselves resist,
we lock it in our memories but still it does persist.

The silent, secret universe of the one true Lord our God
that calls us in our very soul to reach out and break the
curse
that Adam did release on us the day he let in sin.
I must reach out to truth and trust
that in Jesus now I can enter in.

So that is what my heart was searching for,
that Universal mystery behind an open door.
The love of Jesus Christ my saviour has been waiting to
come in
to take my hand and lead me through away from Adam's
sin.

The Age of Faith
Part Two

When I first moved to East Sussex my eldest daughter
started a school right next to this castle.
We had to walk through the grounds of the castle to get
to the school and I really came to love the peaceful
and somewhat haunting atmosphere that it evoked.

Pevensey Castle

Brick and stone
spirit and bone
Roman Fort and Norman home.
Walls have ears so I am told
but this castle has eyes
that can see through your soul.
It has seen many ages
It has seen many wars
It has seen many people pass through its doors.
They come to take a peep into the past
but they don't seem to realize
the future is taking over fast.
Its stony face in the form of turrets and slits
quietly looks on as it patiently sits
and watches this peaceful pocket of life
oblivious of outside's trouble and strife.
Its grounds are eerily silent and still
and the whole atmosphere is somehow surreal.
The ancient ghosts that it embraced and protected
live on in the walls and the lives of
the Historians who inspect it.

The Waters of Life

My life is moving like a flowing river
constantly cutting through a path,
it demonstrates a myriad emotions,
it knows that nothing ever lasts.
A quiet stream may trickle slow and easy,
its calm and gentle whisper
penetrates my dreams.
And yet nothing quite so simple
seems to please me
and nothing quite so complex
seems to tease.
As that sleepy river starts to awaken
and rocks and rapids introduce a change of pace,
I feel my senses sharpen, am I mistaken?
Is my life a river or a race?
And as the rush of water nears its final goal
the energy of my life-force takes a turn,
then suddenly the sum of all my parts are whole,
I feel there is little left I need to learn.
Finally the river finds the ocean,
its vast expanse sets my spirit free
and now I know my mind is open
as the waters of my life mingle with the sea.
So now my soul is moving with the tides of my emotions
I'm free to ebb and flow in gentle waves
and I know now that my devotion
to my children and my life behaves
just like the ever changing, ever flowing
gentle river travelling towards the sea
and the waters of my life are ever changing
to suit whatever form it may decide to be.

A Box inside a box

I'd walked that road a thousand times
my children happy by my side,
we'd passed the building and the signs
that welcomed all to come inside.

But I'd avert my eyes from them
and walk on by and hurry home
and close my door and close my heart, then
sit and think no more about that place and feel somehow
alone.

And I was happy with my life,
my children filling me with joy,
but cutting like the sharpest knife
the stillness of that lonely place deep inside my soul.

Every day we passed it by and gave it not a second thought
and looked at shops and cars and ground and sky
but not that place, no! In that net I swore I wouldn't be
caught.

And then one day as we passed that building,
a man sitting on the wall greeted us with one huge smile
and invited us to come on in,
just like that - but my heart spat denial!

I smiled and declined his polite invitation,
"I'm in a hurry to get home." I remember lying
and was filled with shock and indignation
at his what I thought presumptuous way of trying
to catch a fish or two or three -
my two daughters and me.

So I continued to walk on by
and tried my best not to catch his eye.
And then my daughter, caught with the thought
of having her face painted,
whined and whinged all the way to the corner shop.

I tried to substitute her desire with sweets, tainted
with a bribe and I suddenly realised and had to stop.
And then a strange occurrence,
a small, still, quiet voice said, 'turn around!'
and so I did and went in search of some assurance
that this 'inside information' was sound.

Into the church, that simple building,
like a box of unknown wonder,
with no ribbons, frills or gilding
where from no souls are sent asunder
we found a welcome full of light
that took away the fear of night
and opened up a box of delights
that sent my spirit soaring to greater heights.

And it felt like I was being torn
by two quite equal but opposing forces,
but something new in me was being born
as from one life my soul now divorces.

And then I couldn't keep away,
the children too were truly hooked
and from then until today
into my soul I delved and looked.

And it was as if my self stepped out
from inside the box that was my body
and started then to laugh and scream and shout
"I'm free, I'm saved, I'm loved, I'm me and I am
somebody!"

And then it was as if a box inside a box inside a box was
opened
and still another gift was given me -
and out jumped Jesus, the one joy I had imprisoned
inside a box, inside a box, inside a box, inside my heart,
inside me.

And I have never felt such joy as that which the Holy Spirit
released in me,
I was like a child with a new toy - I wanted it all, the whole
experience,
but I never expected to be quite so filled with laughter,
my body shook with it.

I laughed and laughed and laughed and after
I felt completely spent.
And yet it had been such a relief to laugh so freely among
friends,
I felt so out of control it defies belief but such a message of
love it sends.

I needed to laugh, it's been so long since I've been truly
happy and at ease,
I feel my spirit growing strong,
my heart is bursting and I am weak at the knees.

So now when my girls and I walk past the church,
I no longer see just a building
And I cannot just simply walk on by
without my heart and spirit leaping
from inside a box,
inside a box,
inside a box
that is no longer locked up inside of me.

The Road Less Travelled

If ever you are in some doubt
about your life's direction
take a large step back
and make a new connection

to all that makes you who you are
and to all those lives you have touched
it seems you have come so very far
and achieved so much.

If you observed your own life's journey
from a different point of view
I am sure you would see the difference
you have made to other lives by just simply being you.

Sometimes the road's a long one
with many obstacles along the way
you have met a fair few crossroads
and had many tolls to pay.

I know the way's not always clear
and you often may get lost
but just think of all those you hold most dear
and not of how much it has cost.

Then start to plan a new journey
and this time take the scenic route
don't be in such a hurry
don't follow the traffic just to suit

another who points the way
it might not be right for you
taking the road less travelled
may have a nicer view.

How Great

How great is the love that he bestows,
how wonderful his spirit,
how glorious the light that glows
and the truth within it.

How strong is the hand that guides me
and leads me on my way,
how mighty is my saviour
who delights in me today.

How can I show my love for him
and prove my heart he's won
for unburdening from me my sin
through his most precious son?

how faithful is his presence
that never leaves my side,
he knows my deepest feelings,
when I have smiled when I have cried.

how comforting his healing love
that banishes all my fears,
which are carried on the wings of a dove
to Heaven with my tears.

How euphoric is the joy
that is all that now remains,
in his great love I can employ
the power to shed all Earthly chains.

How humbled in his spirit's grace,
I feel his gentle touch,
that opens up a new found faith
in me that means so very much.

How can I prove my love for him?
By answering his call,
by listening to God's love within
and then by walking tall

and sharing out that healing light
that he has given me
to carry on the daily fight
with darkness, fear and misery.

The Lord is With You

The Lord is with you
when you are mighty
in word and deed.
The Lord is with you
when all listen
and everyone takes heed.
The Lord is with you
when you are confident
and what you do
can make you proud.
The Lord is with you
when you are flying
higher than the clouds.
The Lord is with you
when your enemies
are quaking in their shoes
and all you seem to do is win
you never seem to lose.
The Lord is with you
when you're praising him
for all he's done for you and yours,
when everything goes right for you
and he's opening all the right doors.

But the Lord is also with you
when your weaknesses
control your every move.
The Lord is with you
when you're running
and have everything to prove.
The Lord is with you
when you're lower
than you ever think you've been.
The Lord is with you
when all doubt you
and trouble's all you've seen.
The Lord is with you
when you're running
and fighting for your life,
The Devil is on your shoulder
and he's twisting in the knife.
And all God is asking
is that you listen carefully
he's there inside a whisper
he's there inside a dream
He's where you don't expect to find him
where he's never been before
just tell him how you're feeling
that you need him even more
and he will quietly caress you
and build you up again
he will heal your broken body
and take away the pain
he will soothe your raw emotions
and restore your faith
all you need to do is ask him
and trust in him today.

As I found myself getting closer and closer to God, every day things in the world seemed to be less and less important to me. Yes we have to buy things and pay bills and all those mundane things - but I just didn't find buying 'things' that important any more and at the time started to think there were far more important and pressing issues in the world and my soul to worry about, than what colour lipstick or shoes to buy!

A Faithful Focus

I view the world through your eyes
and everything looks so shallow
as if seen through the wrong end of a telescope
so distorted and so narrow.
Such an 'all consuming passion'
But I wish that you could see
that you are trading in a fashion
of Satan's jealousy.
He buys and sells your soul
like it is a loaf of bread,
you are swimming in a goldfish bowl
living such an empty life that's dead.
Everything looks so different now
I know my eternal soul is saved
and the spirit of God's love shows how
my path is newly paved.
My eyes are truly opened
as the rose tinted glass now clears
and Jesus' love for me defined
the end to Earthly fears.
I will keep a faithful focus
on what is just and true
and enter God's bright new kingdom
I hope with all my heart that you will too.

What Manner of Manna?

What manner of bread is this so sweet?
What manner of meat you give me to eat?
What manner of food to stay my hunger?
What manner of heavenly feast I wonder?

What manner of flakes as pure as snow?
What manner of existence I'd like to know?
What manner of God who feeds my spirit?
What manner of love so divine within it?

What manner of magical morning dew,
that quenches a thirst like no other brew?
What manner of sustenance that keeps me fit?
What manner of manna?
What is it?

It is the knowledge of what is truth
It is the word that is God's proof
It is the body that satisfies
It is the spirit that sanctifies.

It is the love, it is the life
It is the way to finding Christ
It is the hope of something new
It is the law that comforts you.

It is the pleasure
It is the pain
It is the treasure
It is the gain.

It is the food of righteousness
It is absorbed into my heart
It is the spiritual nourishment
that sets my soul apart.

It is the gift that God will give
to all who ask and wish to live
forever more by the Father's side
Just take your fill and follow
our Lord Jesus with pride.

Seven

Seven lamps are burning bright
Seven spirits reveal their light
Seven colours of the rainbow's hues
Seven chances to hear God's news.

Seven horns and seven eyes
behold the Lamb who never dies,
worthy he to take up the book
and loose the seals and take a look.

Seven seals are opened
Seven fates abound
Seven angels carry them
Seven trumpets sound.

The seventh day is over
he has rested for a time,
the Lamb has opened all the seals
and let God's power shine.

Seven golden candlesticks
the churches of his faith
Seven stars of mystery
his angels full of grace.

Both proclaim his majesty
and sing in joyful praise
with seven notes of prophecy
unto the end of days.

Seven voices thunder
Seven secrets to proclaim,
not to be sent asunder
but in John's pure heart remain...

...until the seventh angel
pours out the seventh vial
containing our Lord God's holy wrath,
his plague of fiery hail.

Across the seven continents
Across the seven seas
Past the seven wonders
of the world the angel flees.

To smite the seven mountains
To smite the seven kings
To smite the seven headed beast
with seven crowns of sin.

Forget the seven pillars
Forget the seven steps
This isn't seventh heaven
You're not in heaven yet.

Seven years it took for Solomon
to build the house of God
Seven days of respite
Noah had before the flood.

And only seven pairs of beasts
with clean and holy lives
And only seven pairs of birds
that flew in all the skies

could enter in the holy ark
and start a whole new life,
could pass unharmed through the storm so dark
and start again with pride.

And when a child had died
and then Elisha came
Seven times the child did sneeze
and was brought to life again.

And seven times did Naaman
throw himself into the river,
again it was Elisha's prayer
that cured that fateful leper.

Seven saintly virtues
Seven deadly sins
Seven chances to prove your worth
and a new path so begins.

It leads into the garden
where the tree of life it stands,
where you can ask God's pardon
and go forth into his heavenly hands.

Everything I do is for my family -
I love my family so much and this book
will always be a testament to that love.
I hope my children know how much they are
blessed to have a loving family and a Mother
who will always be there for them whatever
direction life sends them in.

This book is especially for my three beautiful
daughters
Ellenor, Shannon and Alice

May the wings of my love always
continue to help you fly your highest.

I love you all

XXX

Home and Family
Age 30 – 38

A Mother's Love

Memories of a childhood happy and carefree
and memories of a woman who loved and protected me.
She has always been around, so warm and ever-loving,
providing unconditional love, affection and devoting
all her time and energy to her family's needs,
giving us the freedom to fulfil our hopes and dreams.
Only such a mother who is generous of heart,
who offers her children independence will always be a part
of her family's lives whatever life throws at them,
by nurturing their self-esteem and encouraging self-
expression.
There will always be those memories of my mother's love,
of the happy times we've had and the times we've rose
above the little arguments that have reared their ugly heads
and threatened to break the bond that we have always
shared.
However hard life may seem,
a mother's love will rule supreme,
due to her love and adoration, self-sacrifice and dedication
in helping each child to succeed,
with words of wisdom to truly believe
in everything they can achieve.
Endeavouring to be like her, a mother now myself,
I dedicate my time to my children's health,
their happiness and wellbeing are always in my heart,
all I want to give them is a loving start
so that they can be the best they can in all they do
and happy and contented with their own life choices too.
Remember that a mother will always be a part
of her children's lives from the very start,
my mother has always been there to pick me up when I am
low,
she has nurtured and supported me and watched my spirit
grow.
If I can mean to my children what my mother means to me,
my life will be forever happy and full of harmony.

Home is where the Heart is

Our home is really special
it is where our family lives
it is where we share our feelings
and where each one of us gives

a little extra thought and care
for everybody when we can
by remembering to always share
our toys, our love, our time.

By spending time together
we learn about each other's dreams,
each one of us is different
no matter how it seems.

And because we are all different
we all have different needs
and so we celebrate our differences,
our hobbies, hopes and beliefs.

And every time we share our love
by spending time together,
our hearts will warm our spirits
however cold the weather.

Home is where the heart is,
that's what some people say,
so that is why our home is special
because it is full of love each day.

I have always been absolutely fascinated with watching children at play. You can learn a lot about a child by observing their playtime. Children learn through play as well as mirroring what they see in the world around them. Play to a child is a valuable tool not only to enable them to develop physical skills such as learning to ride a bike and developing the various muscles and coordination necessary for healthy physical development but also to help them develop a healthy emotional and social life.

All adults should invest a little time just observing a child at play and then maybe they would learn a few lessons in how to be a healthy, happy, well-adjusted adult themselves.

As George Bernard Shaw said, "We don't stop playing because we grow old; we grow old because we stop playing."

Kids and Chaos

Parallel Play in a Parallel World

I watch the game as it unfolds,
the rules so simple
change to suit each child's
own hidden agenda.

The first child
who had been playing happily
dancing around a tree
is suddenly under orders.

The second child
has hijacked her solitary play
and drawn her into
a mysterious parallel world.

He barks out his demands
of the complicated role
he says the younger child
must now display.

The little girl
obeys obligingly
and puts on the new imaginary character's persona
like a dressing up apron.

The older boy
continues to put words
in the innocent's mouth
and the game becomes
an unnerving reflection of the real world

He sits down
at his tree stump dining table
as she buzzes around him like a queen bee
preparing a royal feast.

Then the evening ritual over with,
the older child jumps up and runs away to play
and the little girl is left standing
at the pretend sink.

She continues her role play,
washing up imaginary
cups and plates
humming to herself;

Then she suddenly realizes she is alone.
She looks around to see the older boy
dancing around her tree
and starts to cry.

I feel like crying out to the girl that
Maybe this is a harsh lesson in life
because when you grow up
nothing changes -

As a woman in this world
You're not allowed to play your own game
because men constantly change the rules
to suit themselves!

In the Playground

Happy smiling faces, wild and frantic chases,
making friendships, breaking friendships,
swapping cards and console game tips.
Making funny faces, having silly races,
playing hop-scotch, fashion hot-watch,
what is cool and what is not hot!
Talk about the telly and whose feet are really smelly,
making scoobies in four colours,
gossip about who fancies brothers
and whose got the prettiest mothers
and whose hair is really cool
and whose meeting who at the swimming pool.
Oh and let us not forget
about that boy that someone's met
and whose brought a brand new pet.
Now someone's gone and burst the bubble
and there seems to be some trouble,
someone's gone and lost their temper
and we're only in September.
Who is that there that's started fighting?
Come on now let's not have biting!
It only was a bit of fun,
no need to go and cause a scrum -
don't fight over a stick of gum,
make up, be friends, don't be dumb,
the school term's only just begun!
And now you see the bell is ringing,
it's time for music class and singing,
now is not the time to fight,
I thought you two were really tight!
Let's all go into class together,
I know you won't be friends forever,
but try and make up till tomorrow,
friends aren't something you can borrow,
playtime's over for a while
but you're still friends for now - so smile!

I often felt quite lonely at school,
I often felt that I didn't fit in with other groups of kids
for one reason or another and I have always found it
quite hard to make that first move to strike up a
conversation. I think this led to me being a very solitary
child and I am still usually content with my own
company. It's not that I didn't have friends, I did,
but never felt like I really belonged to someone as a real
friend, a friend that I could share my deepest innermost
feelings with. I sometimes look at my children and hope
they never have that feeling
of being on the outside in the playground looking in,
just wishing someone would come and take you by the
hand and say "Come and play!"

I implore everyone to keep their eyes open
for that sad, solitary child (young or old)
sitting alone and invite them into your heart!

Lonely Play

Ding! Dong! The school bell's rung
yet another playtime's begun,
everyone is off out to have some fun
Except one!
Another half an hour to kill,
to me it's like a bitter pill,
watch the girls involved in a game,
bet they don't even know my name.
Given up asking if I can join in
their game's for three not four, I just can't win!
Too chatty, too quiet, too fat, too thin,
whatever it is I just don't fit in.
Walk round and round playground land
just me and maybe the teacher's hand
watching the boys kicking a ball
feeling lonely, sad and small.
Find a bench to sit alone,
listen to gossip about mobile phones,
no point me getting one just to fit in,
no one to phone, no one to ring.
Don't even know how to text,
still, no point getting vexed,
I'll sit and talk to myself instead
or that still little voice that's now in my head
telling me to just go home to bed
and find a book I've not yet read.
But wait who's that calling me over
with the crumpled shirt and torn pull-over?
It's someone else who hasn't a friend
someone to talk to till playtime's end.

The Galloping Grumpy Grump

The Galloping Grumpy Grump is on her way to school
The Galloping Grumpy Grump, she may only be quite
small,
but she's on a secret mission to grump past everyone,
you see she has a secret talent and grumping she finds fun.
You'd better not approach her she simply might explode,
her grumping's getting critical and reaching overload.

She's galloping with all her might, her snorting's getting
louder.
It will give you quite a fright as from her nose a purple
powder
puffs out from nostrils flaring and big wide eyes are
glaring...
They seem to bore right into you as if she is preparing
to gallop at full throttle and grump past you without delay,
if you dawdle slowly in front of her you will be in the way.

And me oh my make no mistake,
she will make the playground quake,
as through the school gate she now thunders
and her poor old teacher wonders
what a day will she be in for
when she passes through her door?

But then there is a sudden change
you won't believe it, it is quite strange,
for where the Grumpy Grump once stood
as only a Galloping Grumpy Grump could,
with hair all wild and looking mental,
now sits a calm and very gentle,
cute and quiet, clever and I bet,
a very fluffy teacher's pet!

The Walking Bus

I was getting ready for school one day
and my mum was in such a rush,
she said we had to hurry to catch the walking bus.
"A walking bus!" I exclaimed in glee,
a bus with legs instead of wheels, I couldn't wait to see.
And in my mind I saw the bus and started then to giggle,
A double decker in high heels was walking with a wiggle.
It had a red and spotty dress and yellow curly hair,
I thought that such a silly sight must be rather rare!
I packed my lunch and reading book with extra super speed
and waited by the door because I really had a need
to climb aboard that walking bus, it would be such a treat
to travel to school in such style really would be neat.
"Let's go!" Mum said, "They'll be passing here soon."
I felt like I was on a special mission to the moon.
We opened the door and stepped out on the path
And then I saw a sight that really made me laugh,
A big long line of children was walking past our gate,
They must all want to catch the walking bus too, I thought
won't that be just great?
We joined the line of children and walked down the road together
I met my friend Anita and that was even better,
I had a friend to join me now on such a special day,
we'd board the walking bus together and then be on our way.
I waved my mum goodbye as we turned around the bend,
then Anita and I played I spy with another friend.
But then we passed the bus stop, which got me all confused
and we carried on towards my school, now I really was bemused.
"Where's the walking bus?" I asked a lady in a panic,
"Why didn't you know my dear?" She said,
"The walking bus - you're on it!"
And then of course it dawned on me
why mum was in such a rush,
it was to catch the children walking by
not an actual walking bus!

Hands and Feet

My life's all hands and feet
in paint on simple canvas,
they overlap and meet,
the patterns made are neat but hapless.
My children's hands are pretty
side by side or holding mine
and their little toes so tender
outlined in glitter pen so fine.
And on the hands like henna
the patterns twist and turn,
not symbols of fertility
but a visual mantra
of my family's lives entwined.
I may be all fingers and thumbs
and my life's journey seems to be made
with two left feet...
but each step echoes like native drums
that with my children
the picture is complete.
Like footsteps in the sand
the paths we make change with time
and making pictures with our hands
can speak a thousand words - just sublime!

I wrote this poem when my two eldest daughters were younger, before the little one came along - on one of those lovely summer's days, sitting on the beach watching my two little angels playing - and I thought - I've got to capture this moment before it's gone with the sea breeze and lost to the past.
One day they will read it and understand why.

Two Young Spirits

Two young spirits flying free,
dancing on a crystal sea,
their laughter breaks upon the shore,
their silver voices rise and soar.

Soon they're leaping over breakers,
rhythmic waves like orchestral shakers
crashing down in perfect time,
the beautiful sound of nature's rhyme.

Now they're playing on the beach,
a simple lesson they can teach,
to just let go all inhibition
is their carefree childhood mission.

Whirling over pebbled dunes
releasing dusty, sandy plumes,
chasing, catching, hiding, finding
are two young spirits together binding.

Forever sisters, forever friends,
forever in this world of pretend,
where they will share such memories
of summer's fun in sea-blown breeze.

And two together can be one
under the smiling summer's sun,
remembering when times were easy
and childhood games were long and busy.

Then when they are grown and their spirits are low
their memories will show them where to go,
back to where they had not a care,
where dreams are what two sisters shared.

The Clanking Clever Clogs

We have a new girl in class today
she doesn't have a lot to say
but when the teacher asks a question
I simply now have got to mention...
...she always knows the answer
her brain never ever fogs
she's a fact collecting, thought projecting
clanking clever-clogs!
You can almost hear the wheels are turning
and all the little cogs are whirring
It's like her brain's a whizzing wonder
and the facts come to her like thunder.
Actually now I come to think of it
she's like a robot, well a little bit.
She always dresses to perfection
and comes to everyone's protection.
She always knows just what to say
and does her homework every day,
for every spelling test she takes
not a single error does she make
and every single table's known
from 1 to 12 she's in the zone!
She's only been here just one week
and now I feel I have to peek
inside her schoolbag just to see
if she is human just like me...
...and what's this tucked in so nice and neat?
A handheld computer, well what a cheat!
No wonder she's so good and clever,
what a fake, well I never.
Well Now I've guessed her little game,
I think I'll go and ask her name,
I'm sure we'll be the best of friends
and set some clanking clever trends!

All Clubbed Out

It's 8am time for school and another busy day!
Lunch box packed, homework done,
reading record A OK!
PE kit's washed and ironed and ready for my run,
I have a club after school, a fun run, fun! Fun! Fun!
But let me check my schedule
that's stuck up on the fridge,
I have another club today but can't remember which!

Is it for recorders? Or maybe it is Art,
it can't be chess that's Monday, oh well that's a start!

Dancing at the weekend but that isn't at the school,
Karate Friday evening at 7 in the hall.

Football is tomorrow, I hope it doesn't rain,
Drama is on Thursday, I hope I'm not too vain!

Well it isn't lunchtime bingo
because I didn't sign my name
and tennis I've just dropped
because it just is not my game.

I know it isn't Brownies and I know it isn't gym,
It's certainly not musical theatre, they wouldn't let me in,
because I just can't hold a note
as my voice is not in tune
and it isn't horticulture - that doesn't start till June!

I think I'll just forget it and give a little shout,
I just can't manage one more club
I'm simply all clubbed out!

School Gate Observations

It's cold and the school gate is open
but the classroom doors are still locked.
The children run happily along the path
and into the icy playground to play.
The mums (and a few dads)
stand around the edges of the children's world and look in
through a surreal window of morning mist
as they run off to their favourite playground haunts.
They form their own mini social groups,
a few little girls clapping hands to a playground ditty
and a few boys pretend to be racing car drivers
driving on an imaginary track.
Two girls holding hands
skip around the playground singing a pop song
they heard on MTV and then try to make up a dance,
They gyrate their hips
mirroring Britney Spears, Beyonce
or perhaps the Pussy Cat Dolls.
They think they look so cool,
but it just looks so wrong!

Two boys sneak around the edges of the playground
hiding behind trees and benches,
only popping their heads out
to scare the girls and make them scream.
The parents form their own groups -
three women chat about their little darlings,
about how many after school clubs they attend
and how busy they are ferrying them around.
A couple of women stand close
and bitch about another woman they know
whose child has behaviour problems.
They shoot her parenting down into the mud.
She passes close with her sad child in tow
and the women smile sweetly at her
and croon in understanding tones
when she cries because he's been diagnosed with A.D.H.D.
She turns the corner
and they turn their bitching to a single mum on benefit
struggling to make ends meet -
of course they have no sympathy...
she's made her own bed!
The dad's stand silently together for the most part
watching the children play, united in their minority.
They make small talk about the football scores.

A grown up girly-gang giggles childishly
as they nurse each other's hangovers
with talk of their night out on the town,
their escape from parental responsibility - for one night
only!
They'll still be talking about it next week
when routine kicks back in and they need some carefree
memories to escape life for a bit.
Laughter of course a flimsy plaster to stick on drudgery!
The doors open and the children all come running,
they file into the tiny cloakroom
and shed their freedom and hang it on their pegs,
reluctantly kissing their parents goodbye.
A mother, running late comes puffing along the path,
her son dragging his heels because he doesn't want to go to
school today.
She yells at him spitefully that she's going to be late for
work...
I wouldn't want to stay home with that attitude all day.
The teacher stands by the door welcoming her daily charges
and notes down all the problems...
the parents have!
This one's allergic to nuts and can't have the lunch of the
day, these two are fighting and one mum
doesn't want them sitting together
(even though tomorrow they'll be best buddies again and
wanting a sleepover)
One's too scared to ask for the loo
and one mum thinks the spellings are too hard!
Finally the school day begins and the parents melt away
into their own routines.
The school gate's locked until 2.40 when the school gate
mums and dads all meet again for a brief time -
all part of that unique Passover between school and home.

Not Just a Mum!

A Diary without Dates

I have a book of thoughts,
a diary without dates.
What's the point of marking time
when each day is like the last,
the hours melt and meld
into a timeless mist
until time does not exist,
only on the clock
or the watch no longer on my wrist.

Others seem to rush - to work, to school, to life - but I just
now exist
and that is just my lot.

Now nothing seems to matter,
I'm neither cold nor hot!

So I mark the
passing of my thoughts
without marking down
the date or time

You see it doesn't matter
when I thought them
only that they're mine!

I'm sure many women will relate to this feeling,
especially if you have spent many years bringing up
children - being a Housewife and mother!
Suddenly everything changes and you don't seem to fit
into life anymore - it's a big adjustment to make.

Empty Nest

Twelve years
Three kids
New fears
No bids
Someone's changed the rules!
Don't know who I'm meant to be
Don't know any longer how to be me
Nothing to do but I'm not free
Empty nest?
Just can't rest!
My life's turned upside down
Feel like some washed up clown
No one to entertain...
Painted smile covers a frown
The queen of leisure with no crown
Think I've missed the train...
Twelve years
Three kids
No tears
New lids
For a boxed set of second hand tools!

My Dreams

My dreams are such sensitive creatures
do not stifle them,
they tell me to be strong,
they help me through the long
and heavy days.

My dreams are such tentative teachers,
do not trifle them,
they tell me to belong,
they help me sing my song
in so many ways.

My dreams have such lucid features,
do not rifle them,
they tell me I'm not wrong,
they help me through the throng
of daily life - so that reality stays.

My dreams are such reflective preachers,
do not laugh at them,
they give me a direction,
through faithful reflection
of my youthful malaise.

My dreams are such idle weavers,
do not confuse them,
they weave a lazy pattern
in and out of my existence,
through the silky fabric of my life.

My dreams are such busy beavers,
do not distract them,
beavering away in the rivers of my mind
building dams to stem the tide
of dark and lonely demons brandishing nightmare's knife.

My dreams are such sultry teachers,
do not tempt them,
they hint at something better
and hover just beyond the veil,
beckoning like some lonely and abandoned wife.

My dreams are such high achievers,
do not hold them back,
they yearn to climb the mountains of my mind,
let them reach the heights
to which they strive.

If Life's a Game

Mostly I feel that I don't fit in,

I'm not in the human race to win,

I'm not fit to run and I can't keep up...

...Even if I train to an inch of my life,

I'll never raise the winner's cup

or get the gold, I'll have to fold

and open a brand new deck!

If life's a game I'm not in it to win,

I don't want to gamble 'cos that's a sin,

but if I made a bet

on the hand of my life

you can be sure

I'd get the blunt edge of the knife...

...I'm not the sharpest

I know that's true,

but honestly I don't feel blue

because winning isn't what

life's all about

It's a game of chance

and we're all just taking part!

The most natural state of being...

Freedom

A pure and simple silence
stretched out across all time,
flying through the cosmos
on feelings so sublime.

On wings of patterned pleasure
she glides with open arms
embracing life and leisure
with her sweet and gentle charms.

No thoughts of pain or stresses
and anger put away,
a journey through the void of space
where she can safely play.

And love her cloak of comfort
and peace her warm embrace,
with a heart of just compassion
and a soul of joy and grace.

She is the heart of nature
reflecting all that's right and true,
her eyes a fire of passion
creating everything anew.

Her stature is pure elegance
and infinity her kingdom,
who is this creature so divine?
Her name of course is
Freedom.

**...A feeling and state of being we should
all strive for!**

Living with a Ghost

I feel your presence every day,
shadows on the wall,
dirty socks and underwear,
a toothbrush...something small.

But I do not hear your laughter,
no sweet memories of you,
no photo of our love's embrace,
no mementos of lovers' rendezvous.

The bed is cold when you're away
but colder still when you're in it,
I think of you when you go out to play...
but only for a minute.

My life's a film on one long freeze frame
waiting for the day
when you will unconsciously call my name
in the darkness when you're away...

and remember the lifetime of plans we made
for our children and our happiness
but those visions slowly start to fade
just like your ghost - they're lifeless.

Every single person on this Earth effects every other
person that their life comes into contact with.
They might not realise it but a simple smile
directed at someone having a bad day or a frown
mistaken by someone on the brink of committing
suicide, could have a profound effect on that one single
person - everyone should realise that their actions have
consequences for others and just think for a moment
before you act how your behaviour might effect that one
person you are with at that moment in time.

Cause and Effect

Cause and effect

Force and action

One thing leads to another

Each person's behaviour has consequences...

Even looking can cause a change!

One simple word or gesture

Can cause a heart to break

One promise that is never kept

One lie unspoken but nevertheless true...

Day turns to night and night to day

And lives will never be the same...

There's a Knot Inside my Stomach

There's a knot inside my stomach
and it's pulling at my chest,
every day gets harder,
is this some kind of test?
There's a knot inside my stomach
and it's pulling at my chest,
every day gets shorter
and still I just can't rest.
There's a knot inside my stomach
and it's pulling at my chest,
every day gets darker,
the devil is my guest.
There's a knot inside my stomach
and it's pulling on my chest,
every task gets longer
even though I try my best.
There's a knot inside my stomach
and it's pulling at my chest,
my heartbeat's getting quicker,
I feel I'm on a quest.
There's a knot inside my stomach
and it's pulling at my chest,
the end is getting closer
and still there is unrest.
There's a knot inside my stomach
and it's pulling at my chest,
but God is listening to my prayers
and I know that I'm blessed.

The Journey Continues

A Lonely Soul's Journey

A lonely soul is wandering
through all eternity
searching time and all of space
to cure iniquity.
And hope becomes the banner
and love a torch of light,
the soul becomes a beacon
to herald on the fight.
The journey ever onwards
the climb forever up
until the answer to a prayer
is found within a cup.
A heart so sad is yearning
for peace to fill the void,
until a crumb is eaten
and faith can be employed.
A lonely soul continues
to live and learn anew
until a twin within the flame
steps in to follow through.
And now the soul is mirrored
and loneliness is stayed
although the two together one,
the single soul now frayed...
...becomes a mere reflection
and hence it is not pure,
it casts a shattered shadow
wanting to be sure.

A lonely soul now kindred
stands balanced on the brink,
reality surrounding life -
a chain with a broken link.
The church becomes a symbol
of a key to a rusty door
behind which lies the answer
to all the pain - a simple cure...
...until at last the yearning
is filled up to the brim,
a heart now full to bursting
can carry on and win,
because through all the searching
the soul just couldn't see
that it was fighting for the right
to be whatever it has the will to be.
Inside the heart a wisdom
possessed by every soul,
the love of all creation
making each heart whole.
And only when it's bleeding
can the heart be healed
giving it a life reborn
so love can be revealed.
So now the journey's over
and the soul can end its lonely search,
the answer lay inside the heart
and not inside a church.

The Rat Race

My Life is in full throttle

as I belt it down the road,

I've got the pedal to the metal

as I pull my heavy load.

The road is full of pot holes

that loom up in my way

and every single traffic light is red

just slowing down my day.

As I try to turn the corner

and roll on through the town

people step right out in front of me

which really gets me down.

My life is like a race track,

I need to slow the pace,

Kick back, slide into cruise control

and get out of this rat race.

There have been many nights in my life when I just couldn't sleep and the thoughts would just go round and round in my head, driving me to distraction, giving me a headache and a fitful sleep.
Stress is a horrible thing and I know most people suffer with it at some point in their lives - so this poem is a testament to the daily stress most of us have to put up with in this terribly stressful modern world of ours today!

My Mind is Buzzing

My mind is buzzing
My ears are humming
My heartbeat's drumming
As the night drags on...

My thoughts keep turning
All sounds are burning
The rhythmic pulsing
of my body seems wrong.

My brain's just fogging
As the tones keep bogging
And the pounding's knocking
In my ears and chest.

My memories are mocking
And the sound waves are rocking
And the pulse tick-tocking
And I just can't rest.

My mind is buzzing
My ears are humming
My heartbeat's drumming
As the night drags on...

Money, Money Everywhere...

Money, money everywhere
and not a drop to spare,
can't afford to keep the kids
no one seems to care.

Letters, letters piling up
and spilling through my door,
debit card's been eaten up
and still they all want more...

Frightened of the door bell,
not answering the phone,
can't spread it any thinner,
can't pay the bloody loan.

Trying to keep it together,
let's at least pay the rent,
I'm sure it's not forever,
but it just doesn't make a dent.

Credit, credit everywhere,
but not a rescue plan,
the bank's declined the overdraught,
the bailiff's sent a man...

...and still they pile on interest,
until you can't break free,
the bank gets bloody richer
and then there's little old me.

There's trouble at the checkout
as the last food item is rung,
I thought I had two tenners
but I can only find the one...

The lady looks disgusted
as I choose what to put back,
what happened to the money?
I simply can't keep track.

Finally I remember
who tore it from my grip,
I gave it to my daughter's school
for yet another blasted trip!

Faces, faces everywhere
laughing at my stupidity,
the chains of debt get heavier
until I'm no longer free.

Money, money everywhere
and not a drop to spare,
I'll have to sell the table
but I need to keep the chair!

Let Me Build an Image

Let me build an image in your mind,
a complicated picture undefined...
Shall I sculpt a statue for your thoughts,
a smooth and gentle, tactile one of sorts?

What kind of form will the image take?
Something that will cause a heart to break
and shatter all illusions of the soul?
Or something that will make
a broken spirit whole?

Let me build an image in your mind,
a more beautiful reflection you shall not find
in any work of art that's Earthly bound
or any pure and simple instrumental sound...

This image grows in clarity by the day
and becomes an opera or ballet,
making a pleasant shape and perfect sound,
a symmetry of perfection will abound.

What is this image I describe to you
though simple words cannot explain it true?
No mere mortal could but speak its form,
it is God's glorious Spirit in the dawn!

The Distant Day's Distractions

The distant day's distractions
start floating from my mind
and simple life's attractions
my spirit seeks to find.

I sit in silent splendour,
the day's hard grind now past
and all my pains surrender
as twilight closes fast.

The gulls still scream outside my window
as a pleasant breeze floats gently in,
the moon and stars are glowing softly,
distant traffic noise grows ever dim.

My children are sleeping soundly,
lost in carefree dreams,
my thoughts seem to be profoundly
searching for another means

to capture love's true freedom
from all Earthly binds and ties,
to search out heaven's kingdom
within the silent inky skies.

A Natural Connection

We are a part of nature not apart from it,
we need to reconnect and learn to once more fit
within its natural order, within its Earthly knit.

All life is woven together in a cosmic cloth,
each stitch completes the pattern
like the wings of a universal moth
or the recipe of the perfect healthy broth...

Each ingredient on its own is all well and good
but a single tree that stands alone just doesn't make a wood
and a single drop of water can never cause a flood.

I stand upon the beach and look out across the sea
and wonder how each single soul can ever learn to be
a part of nature's ocean universally.

The beach is made of pebbles all different and distinct,
each one is made uniquely by force of sea and wind
as if the coastline by Mother Nature has been trimmed.

We do have a natural connection to our environment
so we need to look around with newborn eyes
at the fabric of this Earthly tent
and make our time within it - time well and truly spent.

We are a part of nature not apart from it,
we need to open up our hearts and release our spirit,
to fly out free and fly out true and know nature has no
limit!

Love Endures

So much anguish
So much pain,
hearts are broken
but love remains,
how destructive Man can be
to molest so callously.

And to a soul whose spirit's crushed
and adulthood has been so rushed,
do not forget your innocence,
do not be dragged through life -
for time rewards with recompense
all demons' acts of strife...

...And though the knife is plunged so deep
and devil hands will twist the hilt,
the love in you is yours to keep,
your heart so strong in love is built.
Love is patient, love is kind,
to acts of evil we remind...

That love protects and is not proud
and shines on through the darkest cloud
and even when the body's marred
and faith and hope have both been scarred,
in love remains such dignity
and God will bless you endlessly.

For through your courage and your tears
on wings of love throughout the years,
you are carried and nursed in spirit
with comfort, peace and joy within it.
I pray that through your trials and tribulation
your heart will sing in jubilation...

And remember just how strong you are
to live and love another day -
Your strength of heart will take you far,
so with encouragement I say -
Be strong and blessed by God above
but most of all remember Love.

Last thoughts

Ever the Struggling Author

I put pen to paper and try to write something original,
but are any of my thoughts truly my own?
I watch the news and films and documentaries
and I read to stay the loneliness.

When the ideas come they creep up on me
and work their way into my consciousness
and through pen and onto paper...
A poem, a chapter, an idea, a concept -
Is that mine? Did I come up with that?

I click the mouse and fly around the information super
highway.
One Google leads to another
and like one obscure thought bouncing off another
I am soon overwhelmed with too many ideas!
Each one a coloured ball in a children's ball pool
slips around on top of the other balls
and soon the original is buried under an ocean of coloured
thoughts.
Coloured - tainted by experience!

Then it seems that everything I write materializes
somewhere else
with someone else's name on it.
Am I trapped in some pool of global consciousness
that spills into every pen?
I never seem to be quick enough or good enough to publish.
I sit on my novel work of art until it isn't novel anymore -
Someone else, brighter, more privileged with a better
education
and connections pips me to the post!

I send off manuscript after manuscript
and my printer starved of ink dies!
I never hear anything...
Was it that bad?
Do they ever get past the cover letter
and onto the first page
or is it cast straight into the bin?
My poor printer died for nothing!

The characters in my stories
jump into my mind and taunt me...
"You are a joke! I'm not real enough, I have no soul,
why didn't you write me with a heart? I'm dead and so is
your ambition!"

What am I without a pen in my hand?
Unpublished that's what -
Just a single mother with no life and a full diary!